AMY'S DIARY

I'M ~~NOT~~ CHINESE

wǒ bú shì zhōng guó rén
我不是中国人

This book belongs to:

_____

For my spicy Yoona and all the colorful souls
in the world. You don't have to choose one identity.
You can have one or multiple, and it's
such a beautiful thing.

 **FREE GIFT**

As a token of gratitude, I've prepared a special gift for our little ones. Enjoy cute coloring pages with self-love affirmations, designed especially for little girls of Asian heritage.

Download your printable file here:

UpflyBooks.com/free

© Copyright 2023 - Yeonsil Yoo, all rights reserved.
Paperback ISBN: 978-1-998277-11-7
Hardback ISBN: 978-1-998277-12-4

The content contained within this book may not be reproduced, duplicated, or transmitted without direct written permission from the author or the publisher.

Under no circumstances will any blame or legal responsibility be held against the publisher or author for any damages, reparation, or monetary loss due to the information contained within this book, either directly or indirectly.

Legal Notice:
This book is copyright protected. It is only for personal use. You cannot amend, distribute, sell, use, quote, or paraphrase any part, or the content within this book, without the consent of the author or publisher.

Disclaimer Notice:
Please note that the information contained within this document is for educational and entertainment purposes only. Every effort has been made to present accurate, up-to-date, reliable, and complete information. No warranties of any kind are declared or implied. Readers acknowledge that the author does not render legal, financial, medical, or professional advice. The content within this book has been derived from various sources. Please consult a licensed professional before attempting any techniques outlined in this book.

Table of Contents

Chapter 1: Chinese School
zhōngwén xué xiào
中文学校

Chapter 2: The Deal
jiāo yì
交易

Chapter 3: Mission Possible
kě yǐ wánchéng de rèn wu
可以完成的任务

Chapter 4: The Day of the Quiz
cè shì dàngtiān
测试当天

Glossary

Chapter 1.

Chinese School
zhōngwén xué xiào
中文学校

My name is Amy. I'm 7 years old, and I live in Canada.
wǒ jiào ài mǐ　　jīn nián qī suì le　　zhù zài jiā ná dà
我叫艾米，今年七岁了，住在加拿大。

Today is Saturday, which means I have to go to Chinese school.

今天是星期六，我得去中文学校。

Ugh. Chinese school is like a zillion hours of Chinese stuff. I'd much rather be doing all the other things 'normal' Canadian kids do.

哎呀，中文学校里的中文课程太多啦。我真想像一个"正常"加拿大孩子那样去玩。

My mom says I'm a normal Canadian kid too, but I don't think so because normal Canadian kids don't study Chinese.

妈妈说我也是一个正常的加拿大孩子，但我觉得我不是，因为正常加拿大孩子不学中文。

Mom is rushing me to get ready, like she does every Saturday.

妈妈像每个周六一样催我。

"Amy, it's almost time for Chinese school! Hurry up! Get ready and come eat!"

ài mǐ　　gāi qù zhōngwén xué xiào le　　kuài diǎn　kuài lái chī fàn
"艾米，该去中文学校了！快点！快来吃饭！"

I think about pretending I can't hear her, but then she'll definitely come up and scold me. So I shout back, "I'm changing!"

wǒ yě xiǎng guò jiǎzhuāng tīng bújiàn　　dàn tā kěndìng huì lái shuō wǒ de
我也想过假装听不见，但她肯定会来说我的。
suǒyǐ wǒ chōng tā hǎn　　wǒ zài huàn yīfu na
所以我冲她喊，"我在换衣服呐！"

As soon as I sit down at the table, I try pretending I'm super tired.

刚坐下，我就装作超级累的样子。

"Mom, can't I just skip Chinese school today? I don't feel good," I try to sound pitiful.

"妈妈，我今天能不去中文学校吗？我不舒服。"

我尽量让自己听起来很痛苦。

"No, you can't. I've told you a thousand times: this is non-negotiable."

"不行。跟你说一千遍了。没得商量。"

"But whyyy?"

"为什么啊？"

"Because you're Chinese, that's why."

"因为你是中国人，就是这个原因。"

"Nuh-uh, I'm Canadian! Seriously!"

"不不，我是加拿大人！真的！"

"Amy, raising your voice won't change anything. Now, eat quickly and get ready for school.

"艾米，大嗓门也没用。快吃完然后去学校。

If you keep acting up, no screen time after school today."

She gives me her signature stare.

如果你再演戏，今天放学后就不准看电视了。"

她像往常一样瞪了我一眼。

Ah, the TV trap. Well played, Mom.

电视陷阱。妈妈，你真懂我。

She always uses the TV to threaten me. I really don't want to go, but losing screen time is even worse, so I'd better stop complaining.

她总是用看电视威胁我。我真不想去学校，但是不看电视更糟糕，我还是去吧。

On the way to Chinese school, I unleash a mini-rant on Dad in the car.

在去中文学校的路上，我冲爸爸小小吆喝了几句。

"Dad, why is Chinese school so important? Can't I just stay home?"

"爸爸，为什么中文学校很重要啊？我能不去吗？"

"It's about roots, kiddo. You're Chinese, so you should speak the language," Dad says.

"小家伙，这是传承。你是中国人，所以得会说中文。"爸爸说。

"But I'm all Canadian, I swear!" Honestly, I feel zero percent Chinese. Just because my family is Chinese doesn't mean I am, right?

"我发誓，我是地地道道的加拿大人！"真是的，我一点儿也没觉得自己是中国人。我的家人是中国人，并不代表我也是，对吧？

Dad glances at me through the rearview mirror.

bàba cónghòu shì jìng lǐ kàn zhe wǒ
爸爸从后视镜里看着我。

"Amy, you're both Canadian and Chinese. And like Mom said, this isn't up for debate. Sometimes you gotta do what you gotta do."

"艾米,你既是加拿大人又是中国人。妈妈说过,这没什么好争论的。有些事情必须做。"

I knew Dad would say that; he always says that. I give up arguing and stare out the window until we arrive at school.

我就知道爸爸会这样说。他总是这样说。我不再争论了,然后我盯着车窗外看,直到学校。

When we arrive, I see many kids are already there.

到达后,我看到很多孩子已经来了。

"Hey, Amy, did you study?" my friend Mark appears at my side and nudges my shoulder.

"嗨,艾米,你复习了吗?"我的朋友,马克,走到我身边碰了碰我的肩膀。

"No, why? Oh right! We have a quiz today. I totally forgot!"

"没有啊，怎么了？噢，想起来了！今天要测试。我给忘了！"

"Good luck!" Mark smirks as he walks off.

"祝你好运吧！"马克得意地笑着走开了。

As I take my seat in the classroom, I pray that Ms. Li will forget. "Please let her forget… please, please, please!"

当我坐在教室后，我祈祷李老师忘失忆。
"求求了，让她失忆吧…"

But then she says, "Today, we're taking an oral quiz on the vocabulary we learned last time. You all studied, right?"

但是她开口说话了，"今天我们要对上次学习的词汇进行口语测试。你们都复习过了吧？"

Oh. My. Gosh. She remembered!

天啊。她还记得！

I figure if I just keep out of sight, I'll be okay. So, I cover my face with a book to avoid attention.

我觉得只要我别被她看到就没事了。所以，我把头埋进书里，努力躲避。

"Amy, do you want to answer the first question?" Ms. Li asks.
ài mǐ　　　nǐ lái huí dá dì　yī gè wèn tí ba　　　lǐ lǎoshī wèn dào
"艾米，你来回答第一个问题吧？"李老师问到。

Just my luck!
zhēn bù　zǒu yùn
真不走运！

My face turns red. "I ... I don't really know..."
wǒ de liǎn dōu hóng le　　　wǒ　　　bù zhī dào
我的脸都红了。"我...不知道..."

Ms. Li replies calmly but firmly, "Please study for the next class, okay? I'll ask you again next week. Okay, let's have Ellie try first."

lǐ lǎoshī píngjìng ér jiāndìng dì shuō　　　xià jié kè yào fùxí　　hǎo ma
李老师平静而坚定地说，"下节课要复习，好吗？
xiàzhōu wǒ zài tíwèn nǐ　　nà jiù xiānràng ài lì shì shì ba
下周我再提问你。那就先让爱莉试试吧。"

As if I'm not embarrassed enough, I hear Mark and a few others giggling behind me.

gān gà hái méi jié shù　　wǒ tīng dào mǎkè hé qí tā jǐ gè rén tōu tōu xiào wǒ
尴尬还没结束，我听到马克和其他几个人偷偷笑我。

Chapter 2.

The Deal
jiāo yì
交易

On the drive home, my friends' laughter echoes in my head—unforgivable!

zài wǒ huí jiā de lù shang　　péngyǒu men de xiàoshēng yì zhí zài wǒ ěr biān huí
在我回家的路上，朋友们的笑声一直在我耳边回
xiǎng　yǒngshēng nán wàng
响 - 永生难忘！

They have no idea how smart I am. I can do five-hundred-piece puzzles and even solve multiplication and division problems!

tāmen gēnběn bù zhī dào wǒ yǒu duō cōngmíng　wǒ néng pīn hǎo　　kuài pīn tú
他们根本不知道我有多聪明。我能拼好500块拼图，
hái huì zuò chéngchú fǎ
还会做乘除法！

But they think I'm dumb just because I don't know some Chinese words.

dànshì yīnwéi wǒ jì bù zhù jǐ gè wén zì　　tāmen jiù juéde wǒ shì shǎ guā
但是因为我记不住几个文字，他们就觉得我是傻瓜。

Well, they don't know all the words either! I decide right then and there that something's got to change.

tāmen yě rèn bù quán ā　wǒ àn àn jué dìng gǎi biàn zì jǐ
他们也认不全啊！我暗暗决定改变自己。

When I get home, I burst through the door and tell Mom everything.

回家后，我冲进门把一切都告诉了妈妈。

"Mom, I'm really bad at Chinese! We had a quiz today, and I didn't get any answers right. Everyone laughed at me. I can't take it anymore. Can I please stop going to Chinese school? Pleaaase?!"

"妈妈，我的中文太差了！今天我们测试了，我没答上来。大家都笑话我。我受不了了。我能不能不去中文学校了？！"

I add an extra-long 'please', hoping it will make her say yes.

我特意把'不'字拉长，希望她会同意。

Mom gives me her signature look again. "Amy, did you know about the quiz beforehand? Didn't Ms. Li remind your class?"

妈妈又瞪我了。"艾米，你之前知道这次测试吧？李老师在课堂上没提醒你们吗？"

I don't answer right away, but I finally admit, "Yeah, she did."

我沉默了一会,最终还是承认,"她说过的。"

"It sounds like the problem isn't that you're bad at Chinese—it's that you weren't prepared. Why don't you try harder to study this week and show everyone what you can do?"

"问题并不是你不擅长中文 - 而是你没准备。这周你多下点功夫,让大家看看你有多棒可以吗?"

That isn't what I wanted to hear, but the idea of wiping the smirks off Mark and Ellie's faces sounds pretty sweet.

我不想听到这样的答案,但是能反击马克和爱莉的讥笑也很棒。

"What will you give me if I really work hard?" I ask.

"如果我努力学习的话,会有什么奖励吗?"我问到。

"How about that doll we saw at the store the other day?"
I look at her with my best 'please-say-yes' face.

"给我买个之前在商店里看到的那个娃娃怎么样?"我用最"虔诚"的眼神看着她。

"No, Amy. Studying is for you, not for me."

"艾米,不行。这是给你自己学的,不是为我学的。"

"That's not fair! Mark and Ellie get rewards when they do well on their quizzes!" Okay, I might have made that up...

"真不公平！马克和爱莉测试成绩优秀时都会得到奖励！"哎，这可能是我胡编的...

"Every family is different. We don't buy you things just for doing what you're supposed to do."

"每个家庭不一样。我们不会因为你做了应该做的事情而给你买礼物。"

But then Mom pauses. She seems to be thinking it over. "OK," she finally says.

然后妈妈停顿了下。她似乎在思考。"这样吧，"她最终开口了。

"If you work really hard this week and improve on your next quiz, we can watch one of those big-kids movies, with a giant popcorn. Deal?"

"如果你这周努力学习，下次测试成绩很好，我们可以看一部大孩子才能看的电影，还有巨型爆米花桶。怎么样？"

I perk up instantly. "Which movie?"

我马上来精神了。"哪部电影?"

"Dear Princess, the one you've been asking about. It's for kids who are a little older, but I think you'll have earned it."

"《亲爱的公主》,你一直想看的那部。本来只有大孩子才能看,但我觉得你可以做到。"

"Deal!" I shout. We shake hands, and I run into my room to grab my Chinese book.

"成交！"我大喊道。我们握了手，然后我就冲进房间学中文。

It's time to get to work.

该学习了。

Chapter 3.

Mission Possible
kě　yǐ　wánchéng　de　rèn wu
可以完成的任务

The more I try to focus on my Chinese book, the more mixed up I feel. Why can't I remember anything? Ugh, it's so annoying!

suīrán wǒ　nǔlì jízhōng　jīnglì xué zhōngwén　dàn gǎnjué gèng hùnluàn le
虽然我努力集中精力学中文，但感觉更混乱了。
wǒ zěnme shénme dōu jì bù zhù　āiyā　zhēnshì tài fánrén le
我怎么什么都记不住？哎呀，真是太烦人了！

After a while, I slowly make my way to where Mom is reading. "Mom, I don't wanna watch the big-kids movie anymore." I blurt out.

guò le　yìhuìer　wǒ mànmànzǒu dào māma nàbiān　māma
过了一会儿，我慢慢走到妈妈那边。"妈妈，
wǒ bùxiǎng kàn dà háizi diànyǐng le　wǒ tuōkǒuérchū dì shuō
我不想看大孩子电影了。"我脱口而出地说。

She looks up, surprised. "Why did you change your mind?"
tā chī jīng dì tái qǐ tóu　nǐ zěnme biàn guà le
她吃惊地抬起头。"你怎么变卦了？"

"I don't think I'm good at Chinese…" I mumble.

"我觉得自己不擅长学中文…" 我小声低语道。

"Amy, you can't know if you're good at something unless you've really tried. Is it too hard studying by yourself?" she asks softly.

"艾米,只有当你真正尽力了,才知道自己是不是擅长。自学是不是太难了?" 她温柔地问道。

I just nod. I hate admitting I need help.

我点了点头。虽然我不想承认我需要帮助。

Mom smiles. "How about we try it together? I used a cool trick when I was learning English.

妈妈笑了。"我们一起努力怎么样?我以前学英语时用过一个小妙招。

We'll write down the words, draw silly pictures, and put them up all around the house. How does that sound?"

我们把文字写下来,画出乱七八糟的图画,把它们放在房子里的各个地方。怎么样?"

The idea seems pretty cool, so I nod eagerly.

zhè ge zhǔ yì tīng qǐ lái hěn kù　wǒ gǎn jǐn diǎn tóu
这个主意听起来很酷，我赶紧点头。

We start right away. We write down Chinese words, draw silly pictures, and stick them everywhere: on the fridge, the microwave, even the toilet seat! I have to admit it's pretty fun.

wǒmen mǎshàng kāishǐ　xiě xiàwén zì　huàtú　zhān de dàochù dōushì
我们马上开始。写下文字，画图，粘的到处都是：
bīngxiāng　wēibōlú　shènzhì mǎtǒng shàng　wǒ juéde zhēnshì tài yǒu qù le
冰箱、微波炉、甚至马桶上！我觉得真是太有趣了。

Every time I go to the bathroom, I giggle at the funny drawings and the words for 'pee' and 'poo' on the door.

měi cì wǒ qù xǐ shǒu jiān　dū huì duì zhe ménshàng de　niào niào　hé　chòu chòu
每次我去洗手间，都会对着门上的'尿尿'和'臭臭'
tú piàn shǎ xiào
图片傻笑。

Before I know it, I have all the words memorized.

zài xué huì nà xiē zì zhī qián　wǒ dōu yǐ jīng jì zhù le
在学会那些字之前，我都已经记住了。

"Mom, these words are so easy now! Will you quiz me with the flashcards?" I ask just a few days later.

"妈妈，现在这些文字就简单很多了！你用识字卡测试我一下吧？"几天后我问妈妈。

"Already?" she sounds surprised.

"真的吗？"她很吃惊。

"Yes! I'm totally ready!"

"没错！我已经准备好了！"

As she shows me each card, I know every word right away.

她每拿出一张卡，我马上就认出来文字。

"You got them all right! Amy, you're amazing!" She gives me a high-five.

"你都答对了！艾米，你真棒！"她和我击掌庆祝。

"Mom, I'm not just smart, I'm a genius!"

māmā　　wǒ kě bù jǐn jǐn shì cōngmíng wǒ shì tiāncái
"妈妈，我可不仅仅是聪明，我是天才！"

"Is that so?" Mom laughs, hugs me tight, and kisses my cheek.

shì ma　　　　māmā xiào le　　　jǐn jǐn bào zhù wǒ　　qīn wǒ de
"是吗？"妈妈笑了，紧紧抱住我，亲我的
liǎn dàn ér
脸蛋儿。

"Amy, I'm so proud of you—not only for learning the words, but for your hard work. That's the best part."

"艾米,我真为你骄傲 - 不仅仅因为你学会了文字,还因为你努力学习。这才是最棒的。"

"Okay, okay, okay," I squirm away from her, barely listening.

"当然,当然,当然"我从她身边走开,几乎没听进去。

My mind is already racing ahead to Saturday's quiz. I won't let her forget our agreement, though.

我的思绪已经飞到了周六的测试上了。我不能让她忘记我们的约定。

"We have a movie to watch if I do well on my quiz this Saturday, right Mom?"

"妈妈,如果这个周六我的测试成绩很好,我们要看电影的,对吧?"

"Okie dokie!" Mom pinches my cheek. I usually don't like that, but this time it's okay.

nà dāngrán lā　　　māmā niē le niē wǒ de liǎndàn　tōngcháng
"那当然啦！"妈妈捏了捏我的脸蛋。通常
wǒ bù xǐhuan zhèyàng　　dàn jīntiān lìwài
我不喜欢这样，但今天例外。

Smiling to myself, I think, 'Mark and Ellie, you'd better get ready. Amy the Genius is coming for you!'

wǒ xiào zhe duì　　zìjǐ　shuō　　　mǎkè　hé　àilì　　　nǐmen zuòhǎo
我笑着对自己说，"马克和爱莉，你们做好
zhǔnbèi ba　　tiāncái àimǐ yào chāoguò nǐmen le
准备吧。天才艾米要超过你们了！

Chapter 4.
The Day of the Quiz

cèshì dàngtiān
测试当天

On Saturday morning, I pop out of bed even before the clock strikes 7:30.

xīng qī liù zǎoshang   wǒ zài   zhī qián jiù tiào xià le chuáng
星期六早上，我在7:30之前就跳下了床。

It's QUIZ DAY! I jump into my clothes, and dash into the living room where Mom and Dad are preparing breakfast.

cè shì rì   wǒ fēi kuài dì chuānshàng yī fú   chōng jìn kè tīng   bàba
测试日！我飞快地穿上衣服，冲进客厅，爸爸
māma zhèng zài zuò zǎo cān
妈妈正在做早餐。

"Mom, Dad, can I have breakfast now, please?"

bàba   māma   wǒ xiàn zài néng chī zǎo cān le ma
"爸爸妈妈，我现在能吃早餐了吗？"

I'm super-duper ready to head to school and show everyone what I've learned.

wǒ yǐ jīng pò bù jí dài yào qù xuéxiào xiàng měi gè rén zhǎnshì wǒ de xuéxí chéngguǒ
我已经迫不及待要去学校，向每个人展示我的学习成果。

"Take it easy; we have plenty of time." Mom sets my place at the table.

biéjí shí jiān hěn chōng zú māmā bāng wǒ bǎ zǎo cān ná dào cān zhuōshàng
"别急；时间很充足。"妈妈帮我把早餐拿到餐桌上。

I swallow my breakfast as if I'm competing in a speed-eating contest. In my head, though, I'm reviewing all the words I've practiced.

wǒ lángtūnhǔyàn dì chī wánliǎo zǎocān jiù hǎoxiàng zài cānjiā bǐ shuí chī
我狼吞虎咽地吃完了早餐，就好像在参加比谁吃
dé kuài dàsài tóngshí hái zài nǎohǎi lǐ fùxí xué guò de wénzì
得快大赛。同时还在脑海里复习学过的文字。

I take a last gulp of juice and ready myself for school.
我喝光最后一口果汁，准备去学校。

Backpack? Check! Water bottle? Check!
书包？带了！水壶？带了！

I feel like such a big kid—100 percent prepared and all set for quiz day! Ha! I'm so good! Okay, not always, but today anyway!
我感觉就像一个大孩子－为测试日做好了百分之百的准备！哈！我真棒！好吧，并不总是很棒，但今天就是很棒！

On the way to school with Dad, I daydream about acing the quiz.
在和爸爸去学校的路上，我在想象考试的事情。

'What will Ms. Li say if I get all the questions right?' I can't help but grin.
'如果我都答对了，李老师会说什么呢？'我忍不住笑了。

Upon entering the classroom, I find many kids standing around and chatting, as usual.

在进教室时,我看到很多孩子像往常一样站在那里聊天。

I settle into my seat and flip through the flashcards I made with Mom. 'I've totally got this!' I think confidently.

我走到座位上,翻出跟妈妈一起做的识字卡。'我都会了!'我自信地想。

Mark glances at my flashcards. "Hey, Amy, are you getting ready for college or something?"

马克看了眼我的识字卡。"嘿,艾米,你要去大学还是怎么样?"

His teasing doesn't bother me—I know he'll soon witness Amy the Genius in action.

他的嘲笑对我可没用 – 我知道他即将见证天才艾米的诞生。

"Just you wait; I'm going to get all the answers right today!"

It's my turn to smirk at him.

nǐ kàn zhe ba wǒ jīntiān huì quán duì de gāi wǒ cháoxiào tā le
"你看着吧；我今天会全对的！"该我嘲笑他了。

"Hi, everyone! Today we're having another quiz."

"大家好！今天我们再次测试。"
dà jiā hǎo　　jīntiān wǒmen zài cì cèshì

Ms. Li surveys the room. "Is everyone prepared? Okay, who wants to go first?"

李老师对着全班同学说。"大家复习了吗？那么，谁要第一个回答？"
lǐ lǎoshī duì zhe quán bān tóng xué shuō　　dàjiā fùxí le ma　nà me　shuí yào dì yīgè huí dá

"I do!" My hand shoots up eagerly.

"我！"我迫不及待地举起手。
wǒ　　wǒ pò bù jí dài dì jǔ qǐ shǒu

She smiles. "Alright, Amy, you're up. Can you read the first line for us?"

她笑了笑。"好的，艾米，你来回答。你能为我们读第一行吗？"
tā xiào le xiào　　hǎo de　àimǐ　nǐ lái huí dá　nǐ néng wéi wǒmen dú dì yī háng ma

I read each word in Chinese perfectly and am about to continue when Ms. Li stops me to give someone else a chance.

wǒ wánměi dì dú chū le měi yígè wénzì, wǒ hái xiǎng jìxù ne,
我完美地读出了每一个文字，我还想继续呢，
dànshì lǐ lǎoshī ràng wǒ tíngxià, gěi qí tā rén yígè jīhuì
但是李老师让我停下，给其他人一个机会。

If she hadn't stopped me, I would've read the whole thing by myself.

rúguǒ tā méi ràng wǒ tíng xià, wǒ kěn dìng jiù quán dú wán liǎo
如果她没让我停下，我肯定就全读完了。

Mark, Ellie, and even Ms. Li's eyes get really wide.

mǎkè àilì shènzhì shì lǐ lǎoshī de yǎnjīng dōu dèng dà le
马克、爱莉，甚至是李老师的眼睛都瞪大了。

Inside, I do cartwheels—Did you see that? I am Amy the Genius!

wǒ de xīnli lè kāi le huā kàndào le ba wǒ shì tiāncái àimǐ
我的心里乐开了花－看到了吧？我是天才艾米！

When I get home, I burst through the door triumphantly.

"Mom, it's movie time!"

huí dào jiā hòu wǒ jiāo ào dì chōng jìn mén
回到家后，我骄傲地冲进门。

mā mā diàn yǐng shí jiān dào
"妈妈，电影时间到！"

I can smell the delicious scent of buttery popcorn in the air.

wǒ wén dào le kōng qì zhōng de bào mǐ huā nǎi yóu xiāng wèi
我闻到了空气中的爆米花奶油香味。

"Your popcorn is ready, madam." Mom has prepared a big bowl of popcorn, as promised.

nǚshì　　nǐ de bàomǐhuā zuòhǎo le　　mā mā zhǔnbèi le
"女士，你的爆米花做好了。"妈妈准备了
yī dà wǎn bàomǐhuā　　tā shuōdàozuòdào
一大碗爆米花，她说到做到。

Dad, Mom, and I snuggle into the sofa.

bàba　　māmā hái yǒu wǒ　　yì qǐ zuò zài shā fā shàng
爸爸，妈妈还有我，一起坐在沙发上。

"How was the quiz today? Did you get them all?" Mom asks.

<ruby>今天测试怎么样？你都答对了吗？<rt>jīntiān cèshì zěnmeyàng nǐ dōu dá duì le ma</rt></ruby>"<ruby>妈妈问我<rt>māmā wèn wǒ</rt></ruby>。

"Of course!" I grin. "I am Amy the Genius!"

"<ruby>当然啦<rt>dāng rán lā</rt></ruby>！"<ruby>我笑起来<rt>wǒ xiào qǐ lái</rt></ruby>。"<ruby>我可是天才艾米<rt>wǒ kě shì tiān cái àimǐ</rt></ruby>！"

Mom and Dad chuckle and start to ask more questions, but I hold up a hand. I'm too excited to dive into the big-kid movie world.

<ruby>爸爸妈妈咯咯笑个不停<rt>bàba māmā gēgē xiào gè bùtíng</rt></ruby>，<ruby>又问了很多问题<rt>yòu wèn le hěnduō wèntí</rt></ruby>，<ruby>但我让他们别问了<rt>dàn wǒ ràng tā men bié wèn le</rt></ruby>。<ruby>因为我迫不及待要看大孩子电影了<rt>yīnwéi wǒ pòbùjídài yào kàn dà háizi diànyǐng le</rt></ruby>。

However, Mom manages to squeeze in one last question.

<ruby>不过，妈妈还是问了最后一个问题<rt>bú guò māmā hái shì wèn le zuì hòu yígè wèntí</rt></ruby>。

"So, do you like Chinese school now? No more complaints about going, right?"

"<ruby>现在，你喜欢去中文学校了吗？不再抱怨了吧<rt>xiànzài nǐ xǐhuan qù zhōngwén xuéxiào le ma bú zài bào yuàn le ba</rt></ruby>？"

I smile at her and toss a piece of popcorn in my mouth.
wǒ chōng tā xiào le　　wǎng zuǐ lǐ sāi le yī kē bào mǐ huā
我冲她笑了，往嘴里塞了一颗爆米花。

"Yeah," I say. "For now!"
　dāng rán　　　wǒ shuō　　xiàn zài hěn xǐ huan
"当然，"我说。"现在很喜欢。"

Discussion Questions

LET'S TALK ABOUT AMY'S STORY!

Wow, you finished Amy's story! Now, let's think and talk about how you feel about Amy's adventure. Are you ready?

Question 1: Amy is Chinese and Canadian, and she feels more Canadian. Have you also felt two things at the same time?

Question 2: Amy's mom and dad really wanted her to learn Chinese. Why do you think learning about where we come from is important?

Question 3: Amy thought about quitting learning Chinese because it was hard. Do you think it's okay to stop doing something because it's hard? Why?

Question 4: What made Amy try harder to learn Chinese? What helps you keep trying when something is difficult?

Question 5: At the end, Amy calls herself a 'genius.' Is there anything that makes you feel really smart or proud of yourself?

Question 6: If you were Amy, would you do anything differently? What would you do?

Remember, there are no right or wrong answers, only your amazing thoughts and ideas! You can think about these questions later again and change your answers!

Writing Prompts

WRITE YOUR OWN STORIES!

Now, it's your turn to create your own stories. Grab your pencil and let's turn your ideas into awesome stories. Don't worry if it's not perfect – the most fun part is using your imagination!

Prompt 1. What are the things that make you special? Maybe it's where your family comes from, a holiday you love, or your favorite yummy food. Draw a picture or write a story about these special things.

Prompt 2. Do you have something special that you're really good at or enjoy a lot? Write a story about telling this to your best friend. Why do you think it's so fun?

GLOSSARY

- **Prepared**: Being ready for something, like when you pack your bag for school.

- **Negotiable**: Something you can talk about and change, like deciding what game to play with your friends.

- **Threaten**: To say you will do something bad if someone doesn't do what you want, like saying "no dessert" if you don't eat your veggies.

- **Giggle**: A light, happy laugh, like when something is a little bit funny.

- **Unforgivable**: Something so bad it's hard to say "it's okay," like if someone breaks your favorite toy and doesn't say sorry.

- **Embarrassed**: Feeling shy or awkward, like when you trip and everyone looks at you.

- **Multiplication**: A math way of adding the same number many times, like 2x3 is like adding 2+2+2.

- **Division**: A math way of sharing things equally, like splitting 10 cookies between 2 friends so each gets 5.

- **Quiz**: A short test at school to see what you know, like a few questions about a book you read.

- **Memorize**: To remember something really well, like knowing all the words to your favorite song.

- **Focus**: Paying close attention to something, like watching a bird through a window without looking away.

- **Proud**: Feeling really good about something you did, like when you draw a picture and everyone loves it.

ABOUT THE AUTHOR

Yeonsil Yoo is a children's author and the proud mother of a multicultural child, Yoona, who is Korean, Chinese, American, and Canadian.

As a mother and entrepreneur, Yeonsil loves to teach her daughter not only about her Asian roots but also vital real-world lessons, particularly in growth mindset, empathy, and tenacity. All of her books aim to share important messages in life with her daughter and other curious young minds. If you'd like to receive her next latest ebook for FREE, please sign up as a beta reader at upflybooks.com.

Explore More Books by the Author

If you loved this book, you're in for more treats! Check out these other amazing books by Yeonsil, each crafted with the same love and care. Find the one that speaks to you:

🛒 **Now Available on Amazon!**

Bilingual Simplified Chinese-English Picture Book

AGES 4-7

Non-fiction on World Economy and History

AGES 8-12

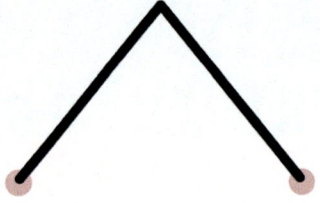

Hope you and your little one enjoyed our story! If so, could you spare a moment to rate the book or share your thoughts on Amazon?

Even a quick one-click rating would mean the world to me. It helps me continue creating more educational and fun stories for awesome kids like yours.

Warm regards,
Yeonsil

P.S. Don't forget your free coloring + writing book:
upflybooks.com/free